Fireball Tim's
BIG BOOK of
Wacky States!

Illustrated by

Fireball Tim Lawrence

Malibu Road Press

Copyright © 2014 Fireball Tim Lawrence

ISBN: 1505242223
ISBN-13: 978-1505242225

DEDICATION

For kids of all ages. May you be inspired to
make the world a better place through creativity.

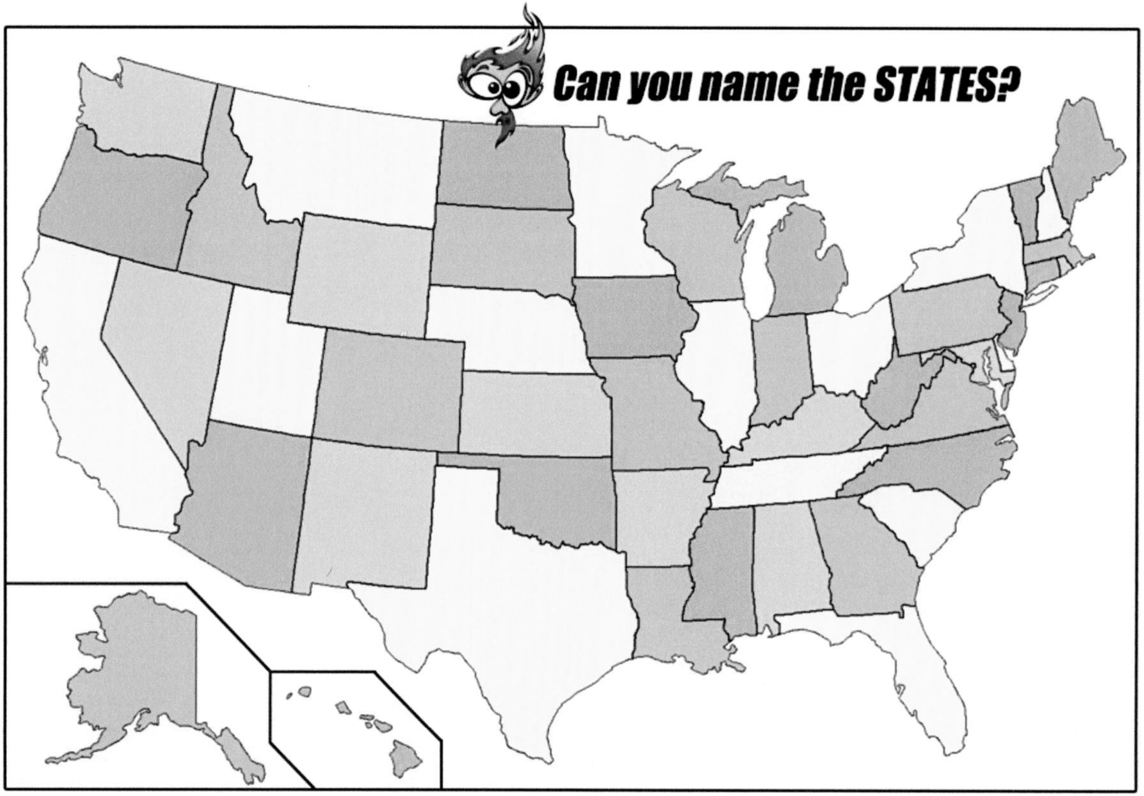
Can you name the STATES?

ACKNOWLEDGMENTS

For my wife, Kathie.
The greatest kid I've ever known.

Thank you.

B'COOL
THE PREZ
ECO-TURBO

A message from our Leader...
"BE COOL,
and Welcome to the Wacky States!"

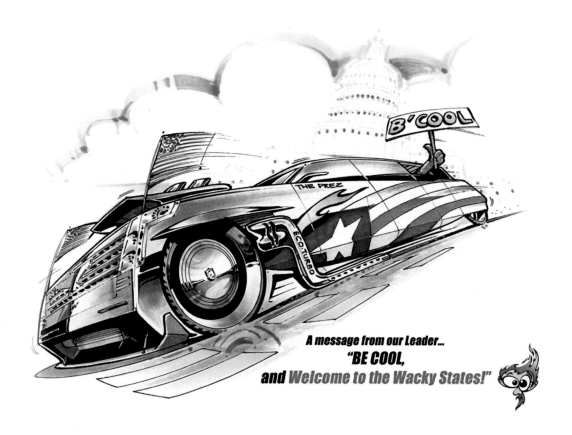

Alabama

State Capital: MONTGOMERY

State Animal: BLACK BEAR

State Bird: YELLOWHAMMER

WACKY FACT! Alabama has 22 State Parks!

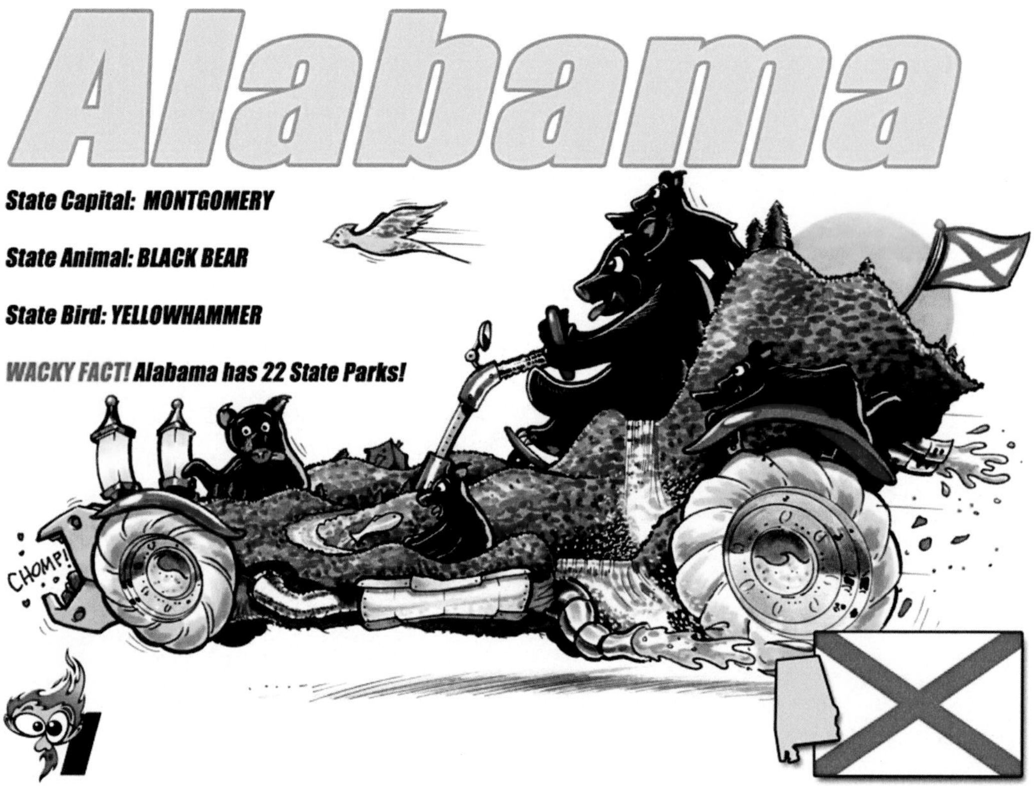
CHOMP!

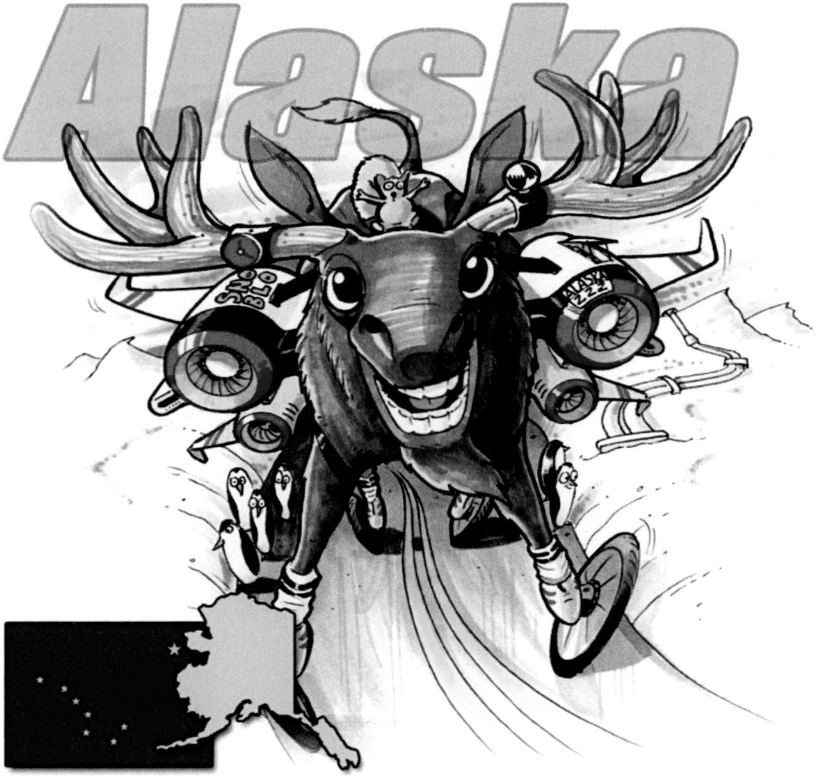
Alaska

State Capital:
JUNEAU

State Animal:
The MOOSE

State Tree:
The SPRUCE

State Fish:
CHINOOK SALMON

State Flower:
FORGET-ME-NOT

WACKY FACT!
Alaska is twice as big as Texas!

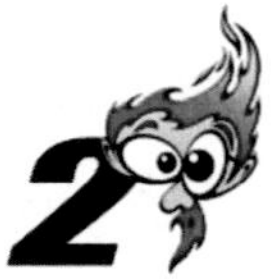
2

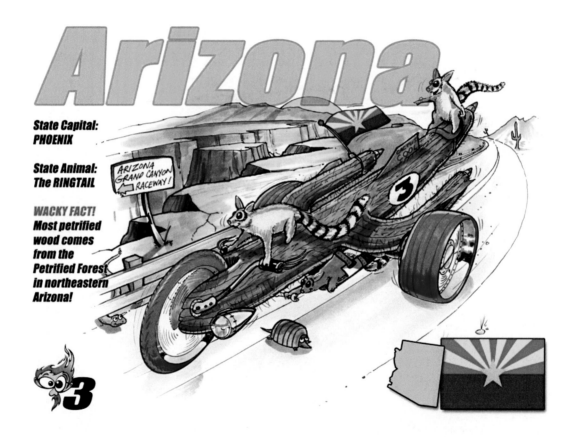

Arizona

State Capital:
PHOENIX

State Animal:
The RINGTAIL

WACKY FACT!
Most petrified wood comes from the Petrified Forest in northeastern Arizona!

ARIZONA GRAND CANYON RACEWAY!

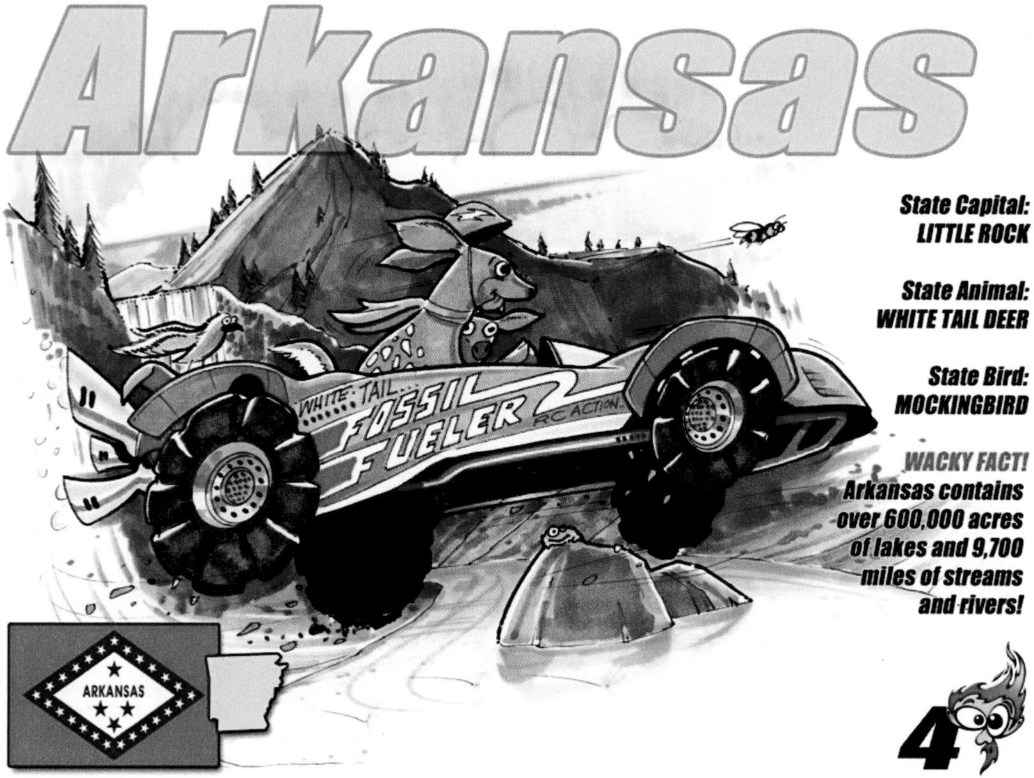
Arkansas
WHITE TAIL... FOSSIL FUELER
RC ACTION
State Capital:
LITTLE ROCK
State Animal:
WHITE TAIL DEER
State Bird:
MOCKINGBIRD
WACKY FACT!
Arkansas contains over 600,000 acres of lakes and 9,700 miles of streams and rivers!
ARKANSAS
4

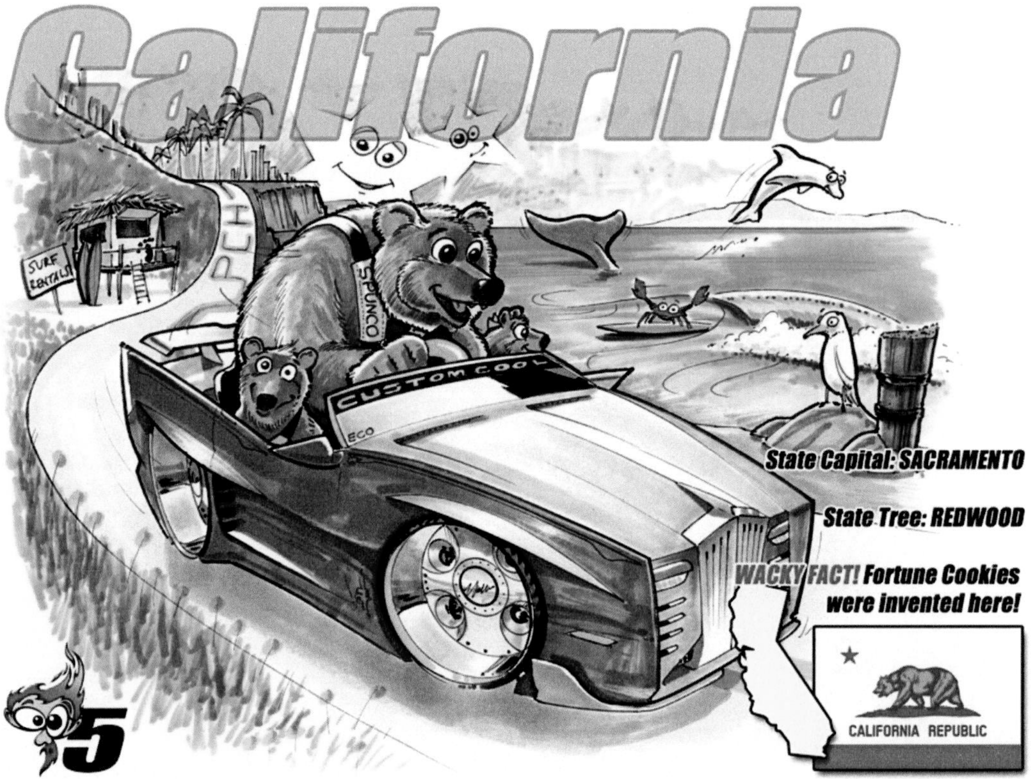
California
SURF RENTALS
PCH
SPUNCO
CUSTOM COOL
ECO
State Capital: SACRAMENTO
State Tree: REDWOOD
WACKY FACT! Fortune Cookies were invented here!
CALIFORNIA REPUBLIC
5

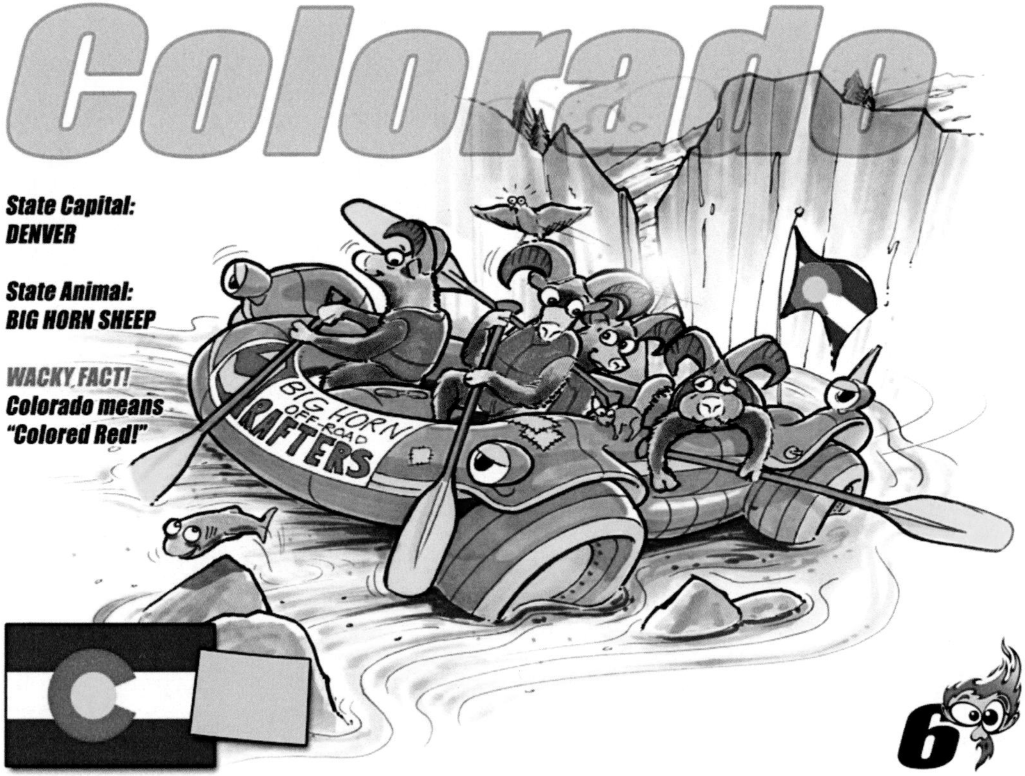
Colorado
State Capital:
DENVER
State Animal:
BIG HORN SHEEP
WACKY FACT!
Colorado means
"Colored Red!"
BIG HORN
OFF-ROAD
RAFTERS
6

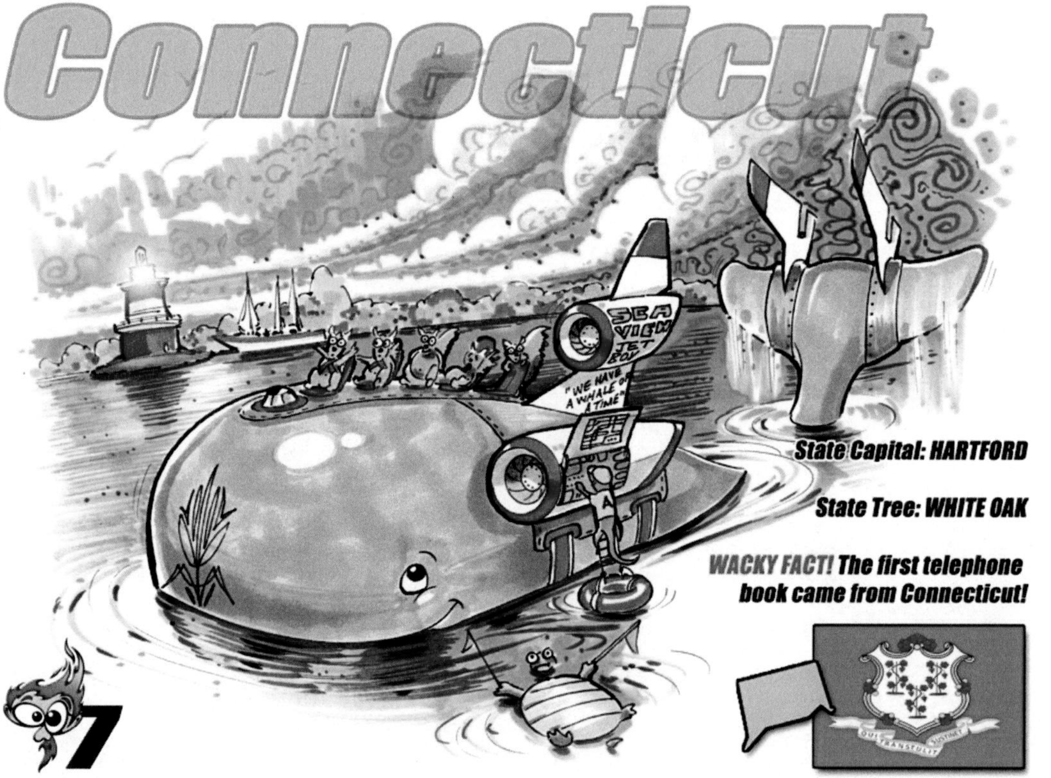
Connecticut
SEA VIEW JET BOY
"WE HAVE A WHALE OF A TIME"
State Capital: HARTFORD
State Tree: WHITE OAK
WACKY FACT! The first telephone book came from Connecticut!
7

Delaware

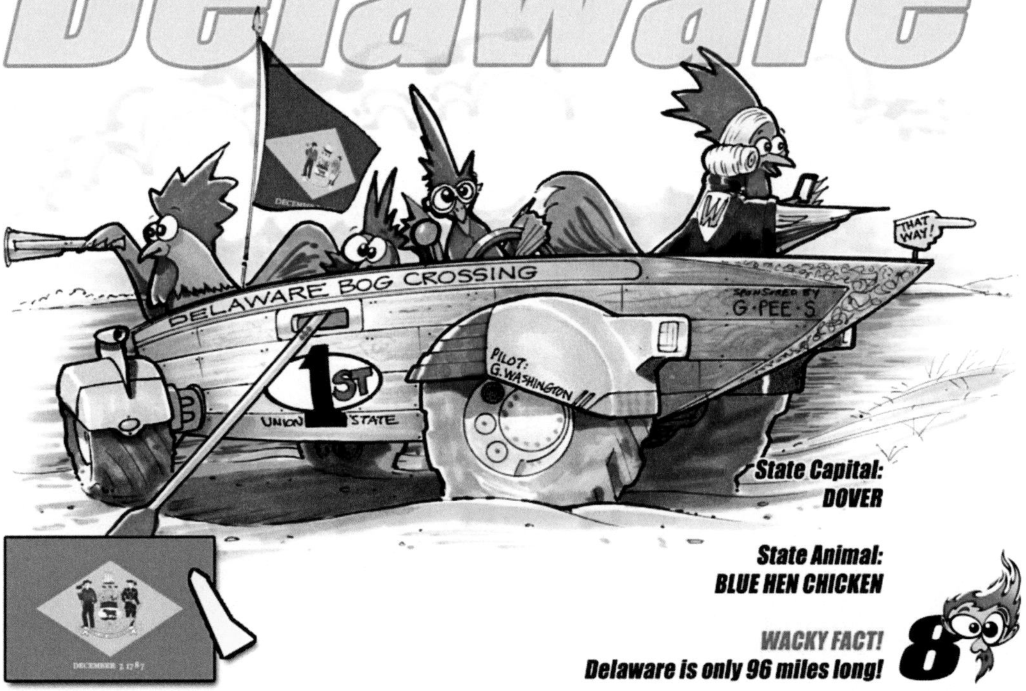
DELAWARE BOG CROSSING
SPONSORED BY
G·PEE·S
1ST
UNION STATE
PILOT:
G.WASHINGTON
THAT WAY!

State Capital:
DOVER

State Animal:
BLUE HEN CHICKEN

WACKY FACT!
Delaware is only 96 miles long!

Florida

State Capital:
TALLAHASSEE

State Tree:
PALM

State Mammal:
DOLPHIN

WACKY FACT!
Key Largo is the Diving Capital of the World!

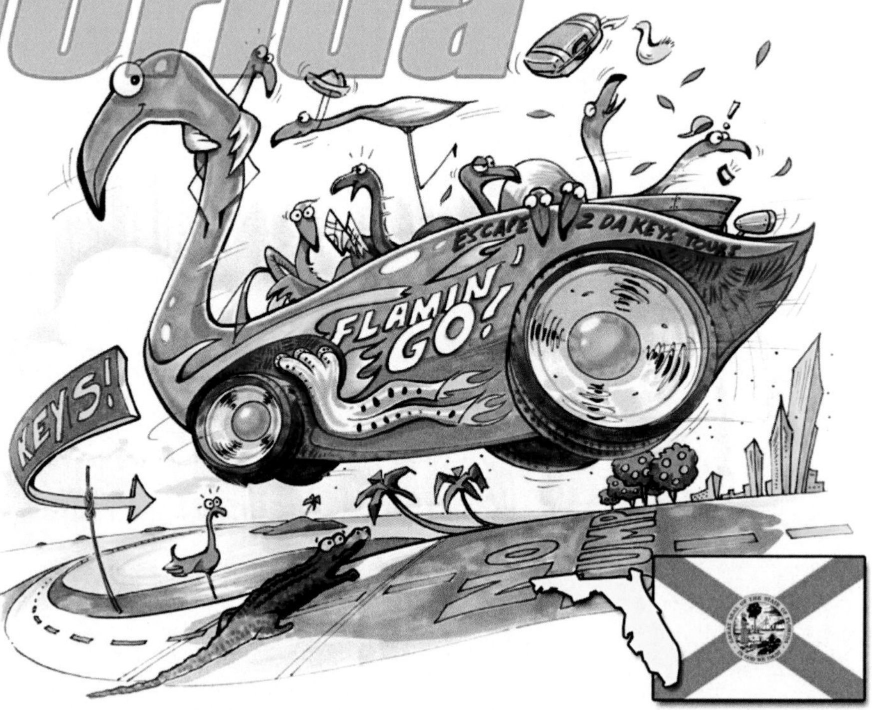
ESCAPE 2 DA KEYS TOUR
FLAMIN GO!
KEYS!

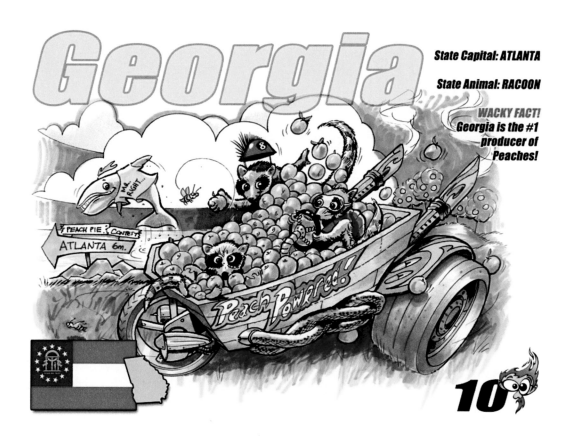

Georgia
State Capital: ATLANTA
State Animal: RACOON
WACKY FACT!
Georgia is the #1 producer of Peaches!
MR. RIGHT...
PEACH PIE CONTEST
ATLANTA 6m.
Peach Powered!
10

Hawaii

3RD ANNUAL COCONUT RUN!
JUDGE

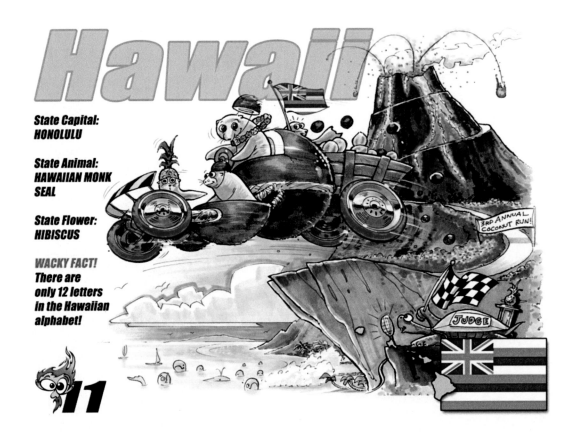

State Capital:
HONOLULU

State Animal:
HAWAIIAN MONK SEAL

State Flower:
HIBISCUS

WACKY FACT!
There are only 12 letters in the Hawaiian alphabet!

11

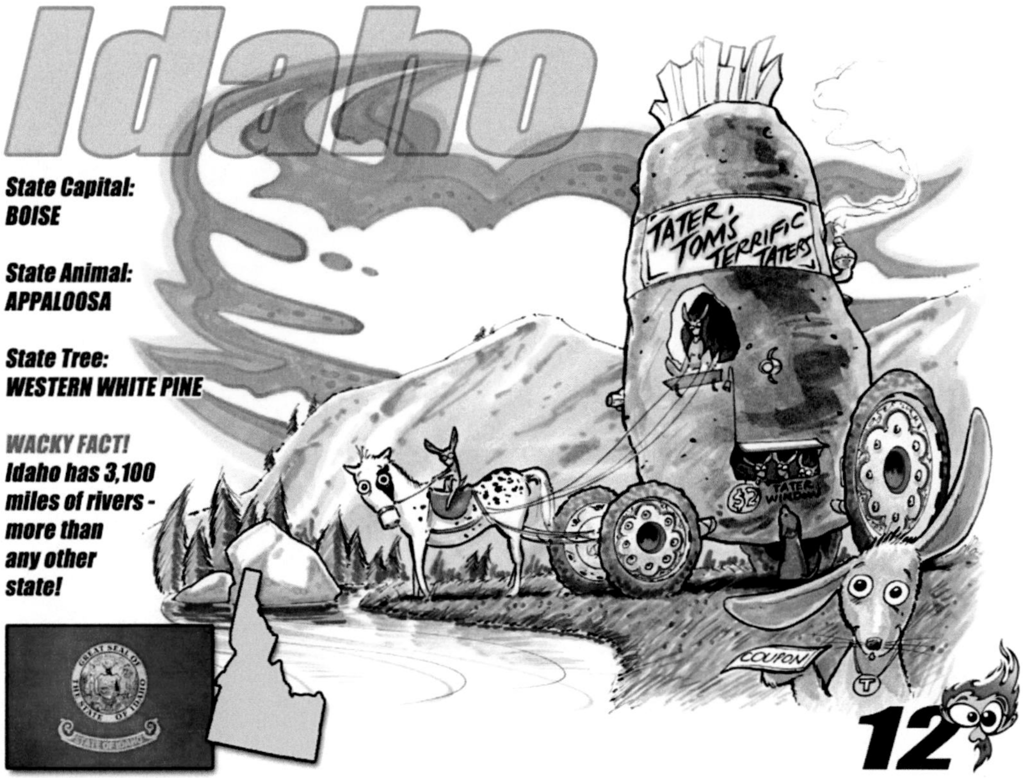
Idaho
State Capital:
BOISE
State Animal:
APPALOOSA
State Tree:
WESTERN WHITE PINE
WACKY FACT!
Idaho has 3,100 miles of rivers - more than any other state!
TATER TOM'S TERRIFIC TATERS
$2
TATER WINDOW
COUPON
12

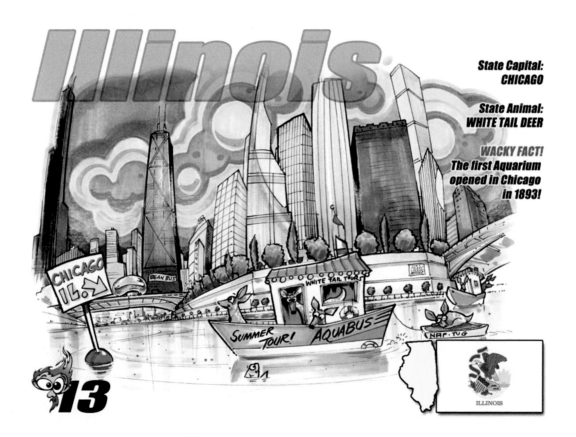

Illinois
State Capital:
CHICAGO
State Animal:
WHITE TAIL DEER
WACKY FACT!
The first Aquarium opened in Chicago in 1893!
CHICAGO IL.
BEAN BUS
WHITE TAIL TOURS
SUMMER TOUR!
AQUABUS
13
ILLINOIS

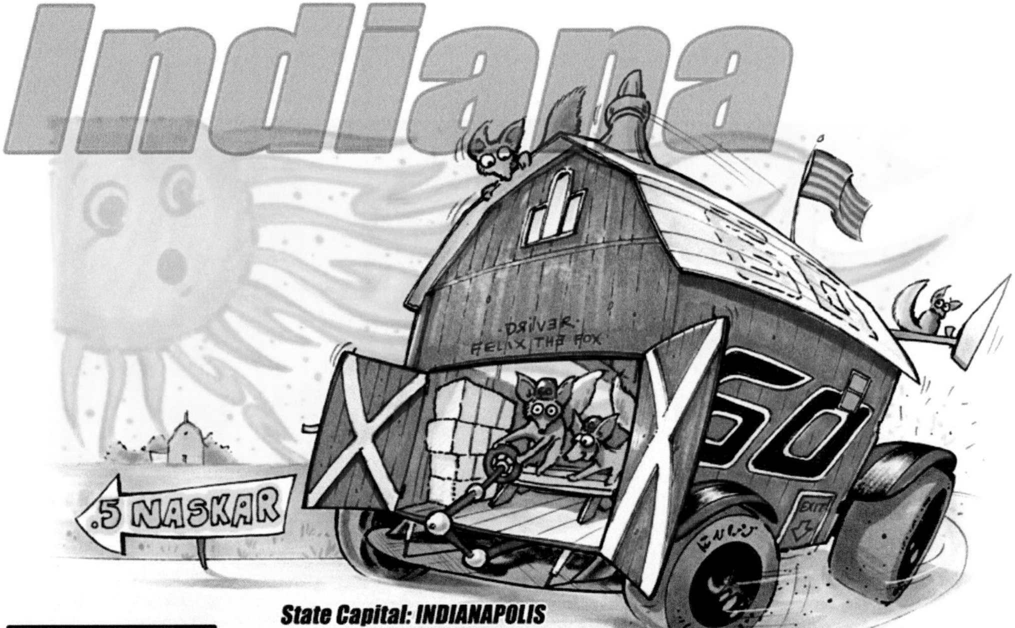
Indiana
DRIVER
FELIX THE FOX
.5 NASKAR

State Capital: INDIANAPOLIS

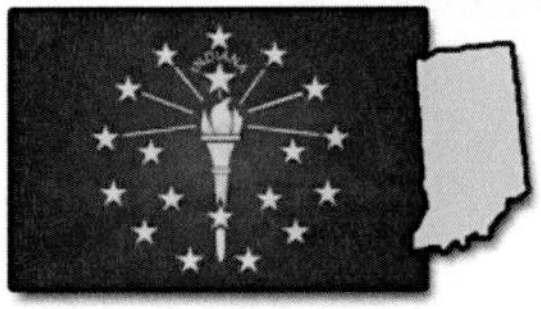

State Bird: CARDINAL

WACKY FACT!
Indiana means "Land of the Indians."

14

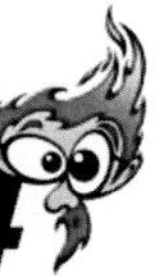

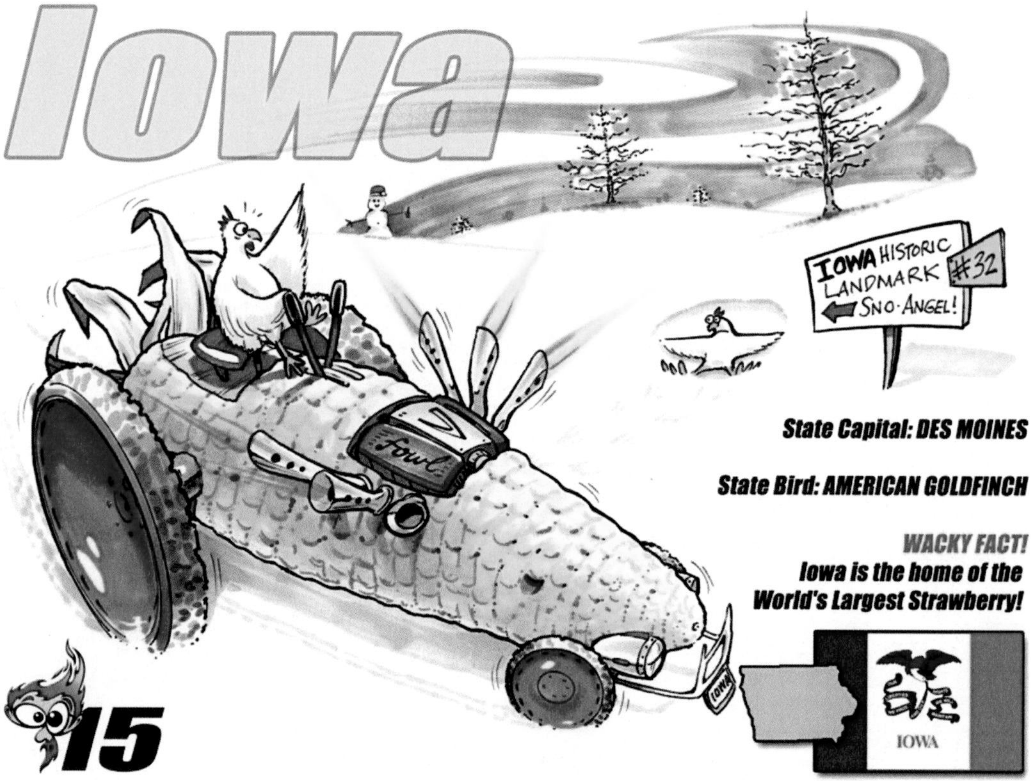
Iowa
IOWA HISTORIC LANDMARK #32
SNO-ANGEL!
fowl
IOWA
15
IOWA

State Capital: DES MOINES

State Bird: AMERICAN GOLDFINCH

WACKY FACT!
Iowa is the home of the World's Largest Strawberry!

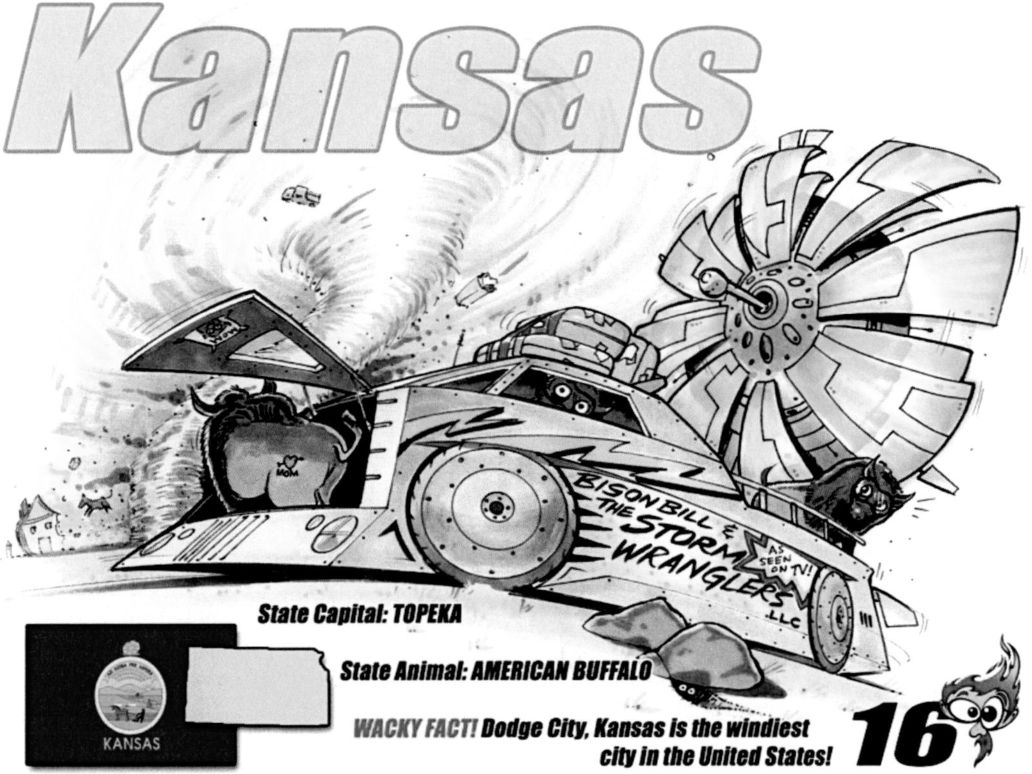
Kansas
BISON BILL & THE STORM WRANGLERS LLC
AS SEEN ON TV!
MOM
KANSAS
State Capital: TOPEKA
State Animal: AMERICAN BUFFALO
WACKY FACT! Dodge City, Kansas is the windiest city in the United States!
16

Kentucky

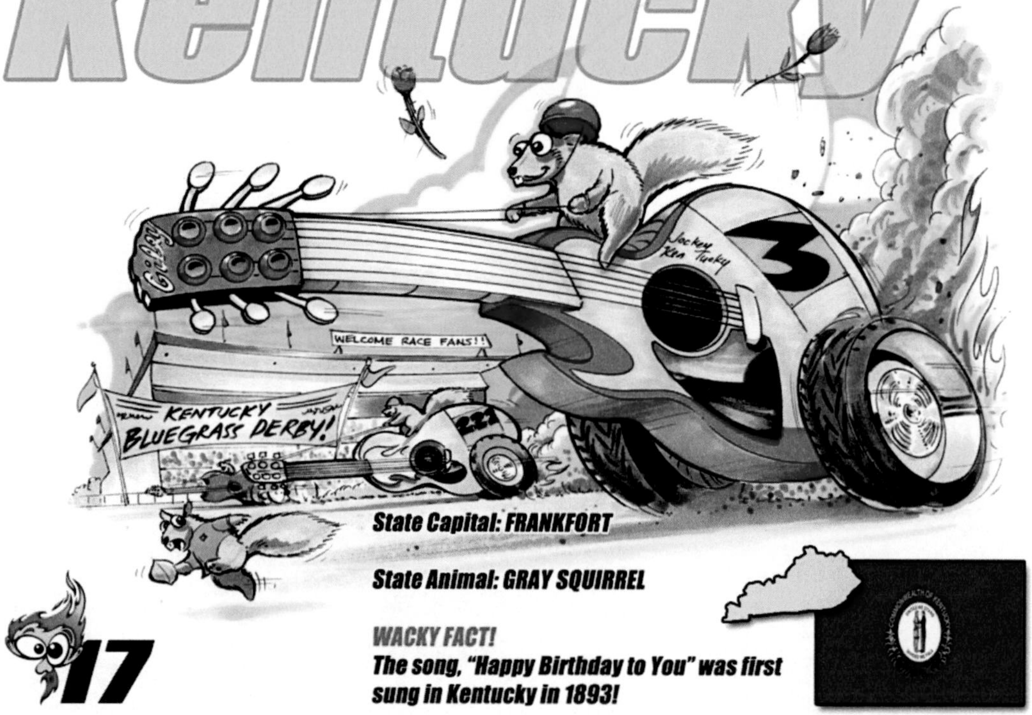
WELCOME RACE FANS!!
KENTUCKY BLUEGRASS DERBY!
Jockey Ken Tucky
3
221
17

State Capital: FRANKFORT

State Animal: GRAY SQUIRREL

WACKY FACT!

The song, "Happy Birthday to You" was first sung in Kentucky in 1893!

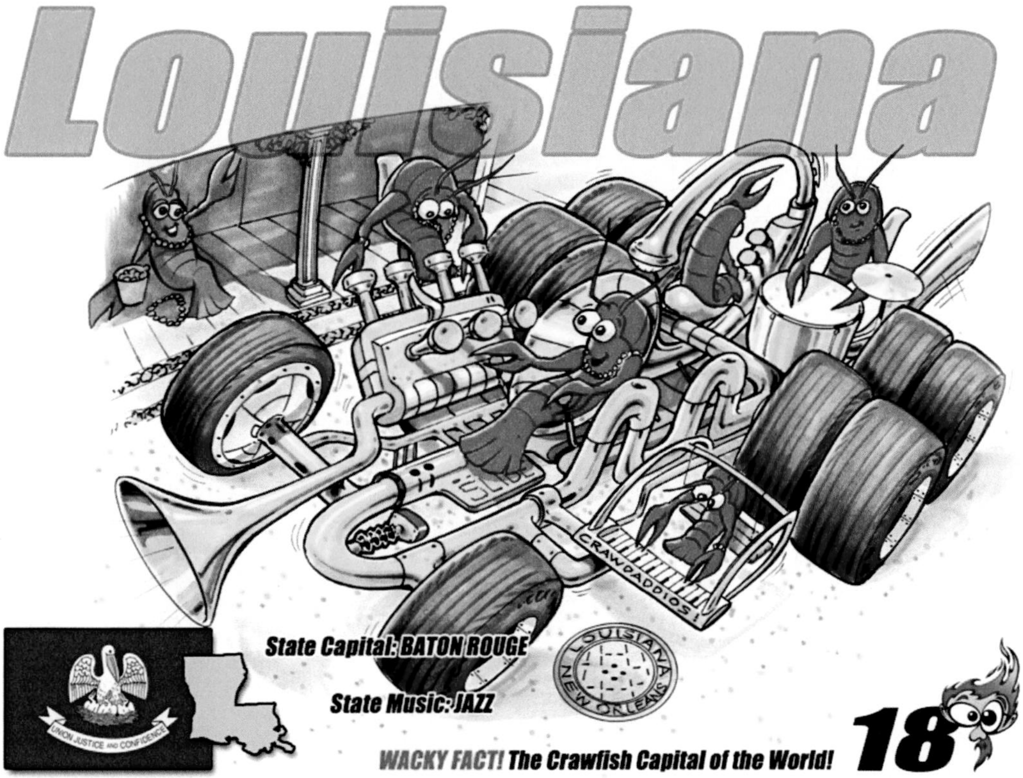
Louisiana
SLIDE
CRAWDADDIOS!
UNION JUSTICE AND CONFIDENCE
State Capital: BATON ROUGE
LOUISIANA
NEW ORLEANS
State Music: JAZZ
WACKY FACT! The Crawfish Capital of the World!
18

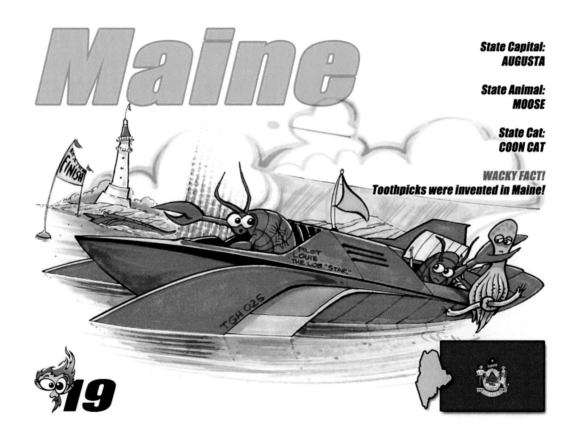

Maine
State Capital:
AUGUSTA
State Animal:
MOOSE
State Cat:
COON CAT
WACKY FACT!
Toothpicks were invented in Maine!
FINISH
PILOT LOUIE THE LOB "STAR"
TGH 025
19

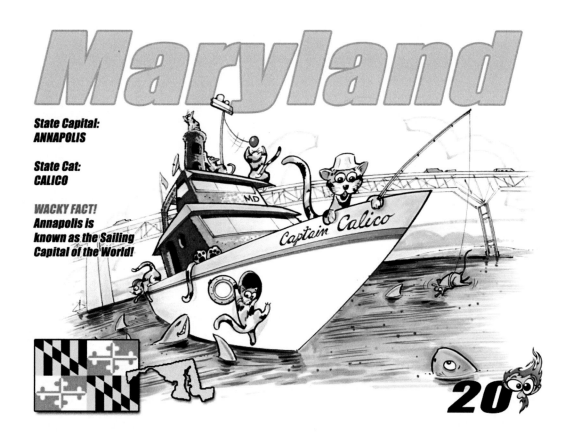

Maryland

State Capital:
ANNAPOLIS

State Cat:
CALICO

WACKY FACT!
Annapolis is
known as the Sailing
Capital of the World!

20

Massachusetts

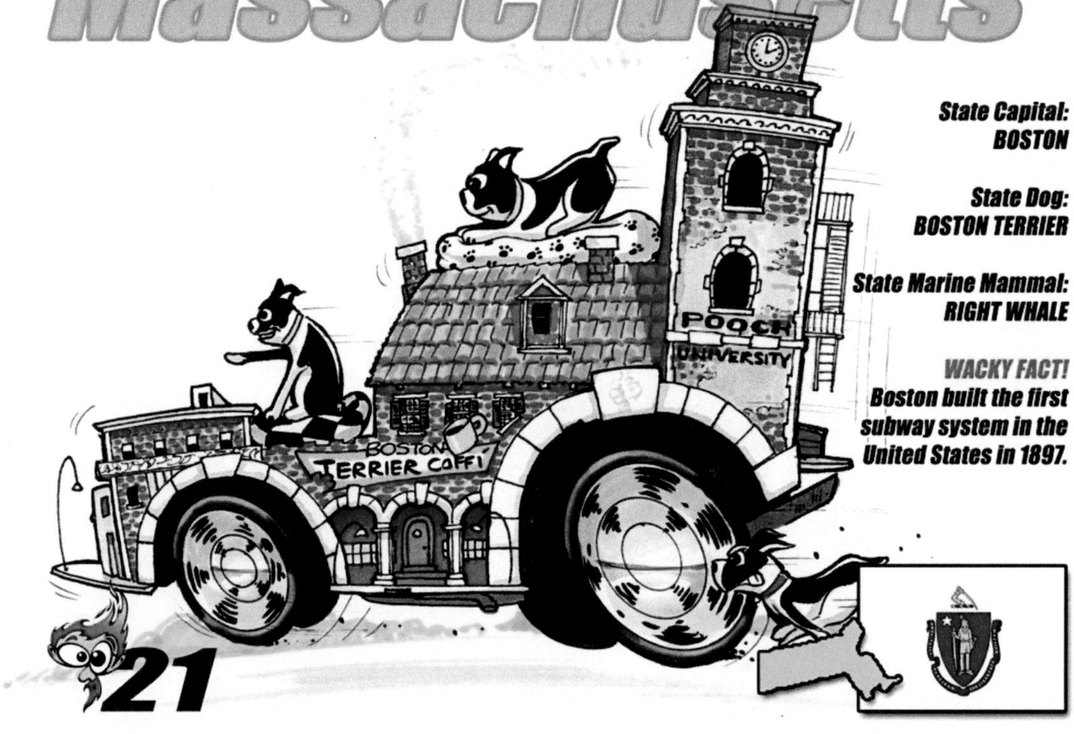
BOSTON
POOCH
UNIVERSITY
21

State Capital:
BOSTON

State Dog:
BOSTON TERRIER

State Marine Mammal:
RIGHT WHALE

WACKY FACT!
Boston built the first subway system in the United States in 1897.

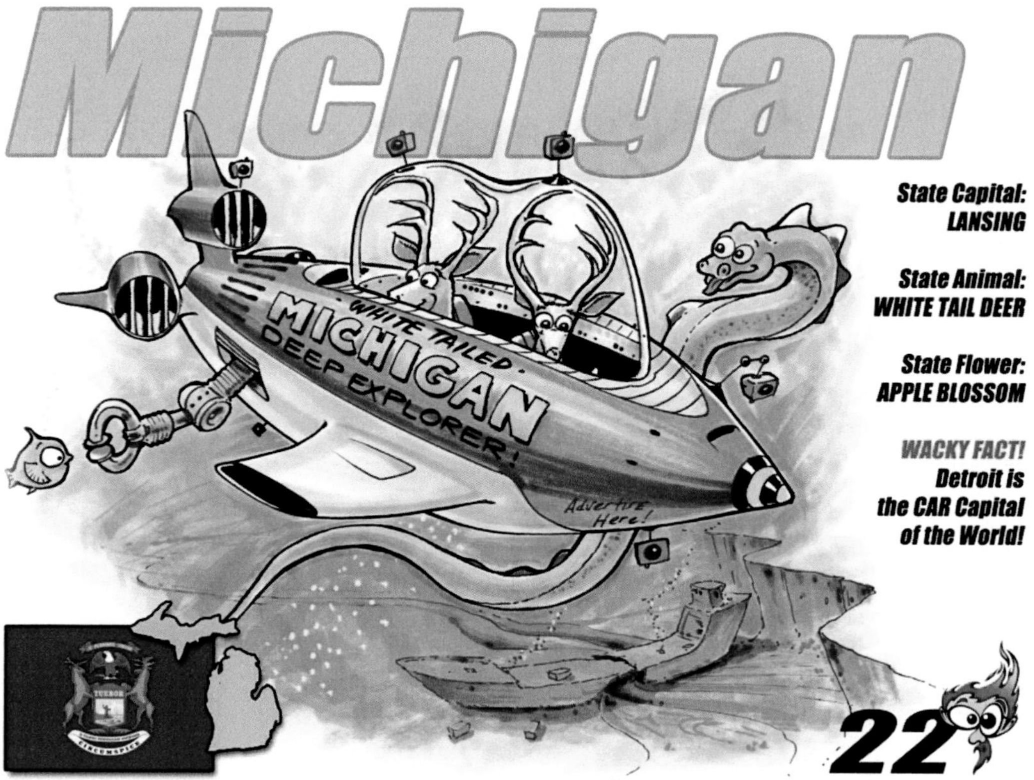
Michigan
WHITE TAILED
MICHIGAN
DEEP EXPLORER!
Advertise Here!
State Capital:
LANSING
State Animal:
WHITE TAIL DEER
State Flower:
APPLE BLOSSOM
WACKY FACT!
Detroit is
the CAR Capital
of the World!
TUEBOR
22

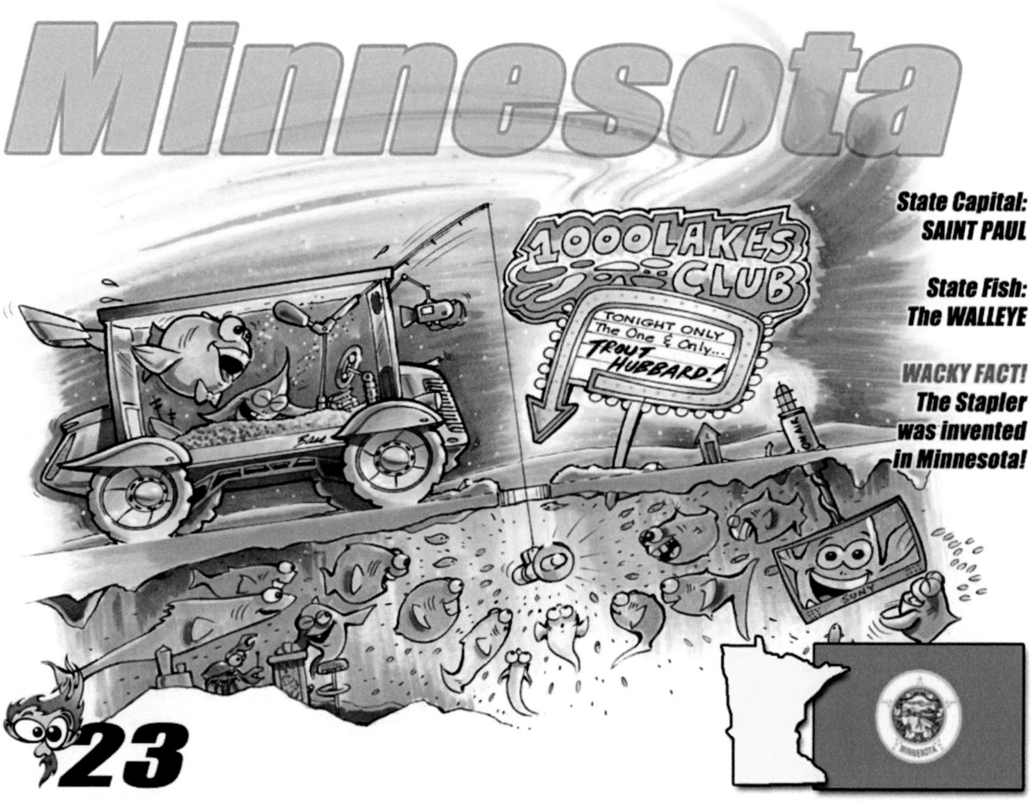
Minnesota
State Capital:
SAINT PAUL
State Fish:
The WALLEYE
WACKY FACT!
The Stapler
was invented
in Minnesota!
1000 LAKES CLUB
TONIGHT ONLY
The One & Only...
TROUT HUBBARD!
23

Mississippi

VIEW
MISSISSIPPI
ROCKET
PADDLERS!

State Capital:
JACKSON

State Animal:
RED FOX

WACKY FACT!
Mississippi
is the Cotton
Capital of the World!

24

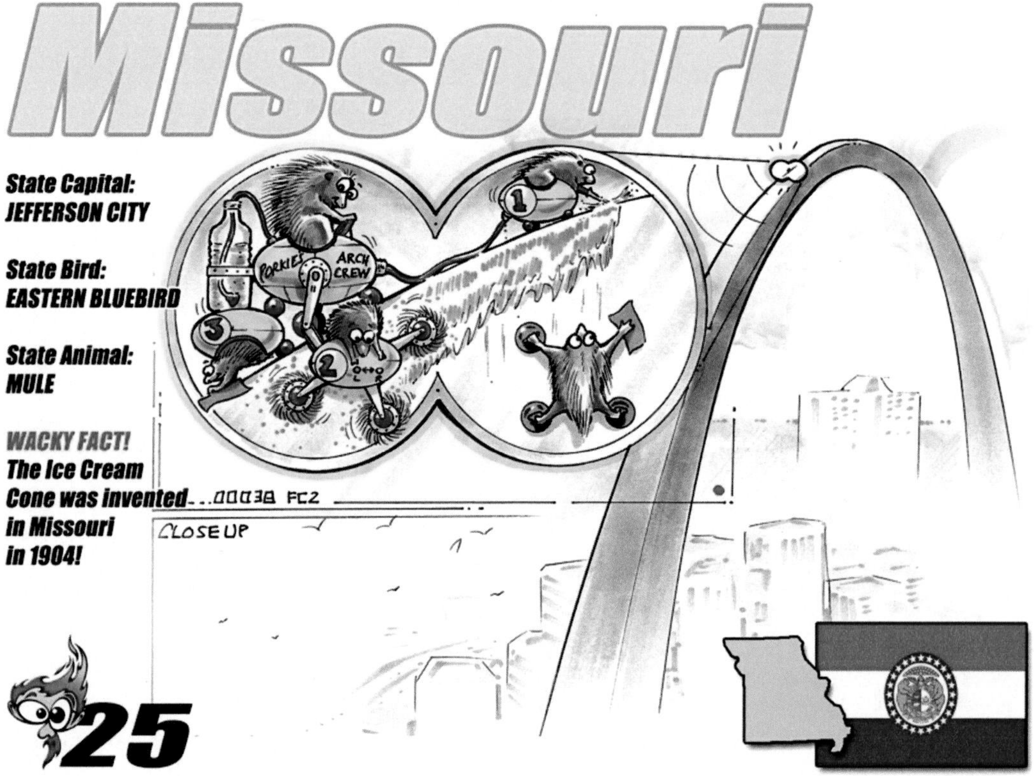
Missouri
State Capital:
JEFFERSON CITY
State Bird:
EASTERN BLUEBIRD
State Animal:
MULE
WACKY FACT!
The Ice Cream Cone was invented in Missouri in 1904!
PORKIES ARCH CREW
1
2
3
00038 FC2
CLOSEUP
25

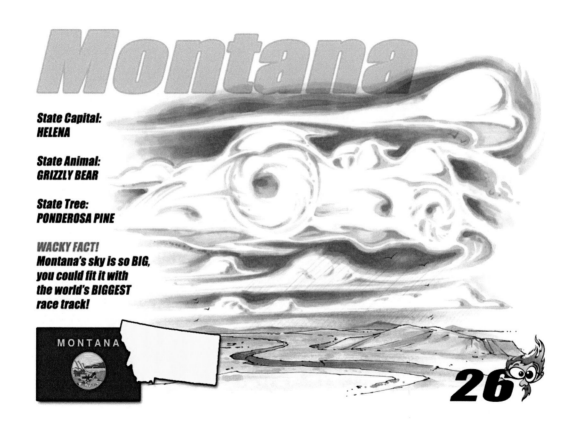

Montana

State Capital:
HELENA

State Animal:
GRIZZLY BEAR

State Tree:
PONDEROSA PINE

WACKY FACT!
Montana's sky is so BIG,
you could fit it with
the world's BIGGEST
race track!

MONTANA

26

Nebraska

State Capital:
LINCOLN

State Insect:
THE HONEY BEE

State Flower:
GOLDENROD

WACKY FACT!
Buffalo Bill Cody
held his first rodeo
in Nebraska
July 4, 1882!

27

Nevada

State Capital:
CARSON CITY

State Tree:
PINE

State Flower:
SAGEBRUSH

WACKY FACT!
Las Vegas has more hotel rooms than any other place on earth!

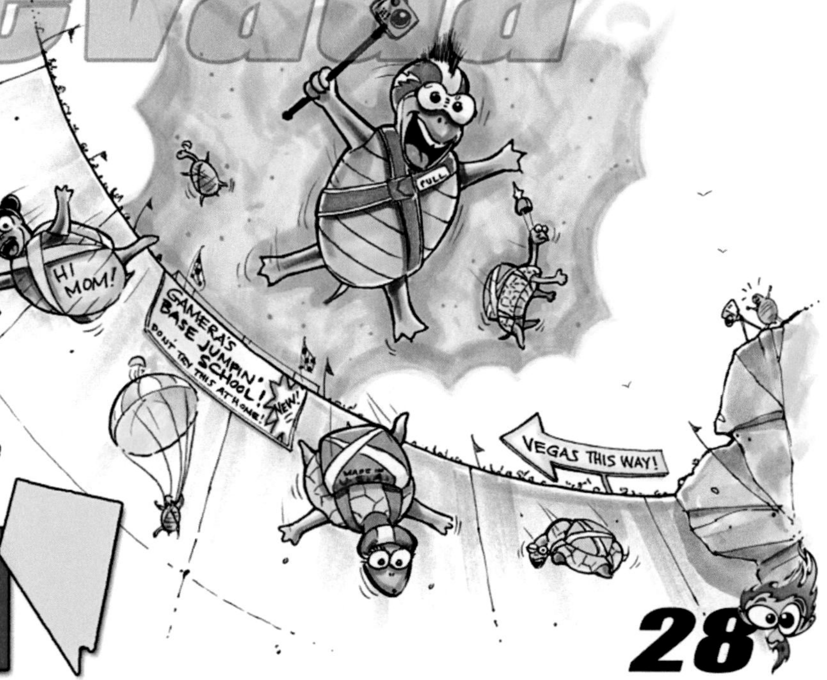
PULL
HI MOM!
GAMERA'S BASE JUMPIN' SCHOOL!
DONT TRY THIS AT HOME!
NEW!
VEGAS THIS WAY!
28

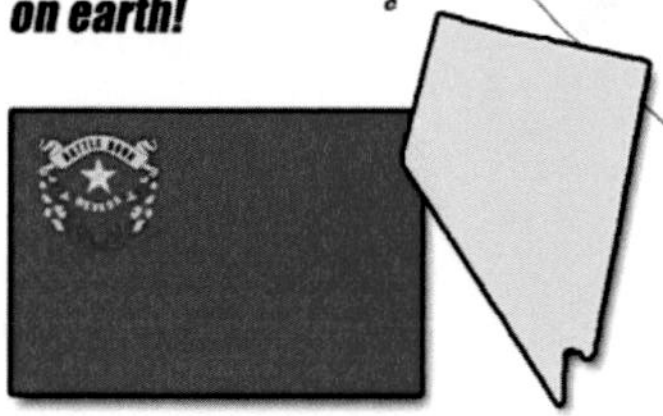

New Hampshire

State Capital:
CONCORD

State Fruit:
PUMPKIN

State Tree:
BIRCH

State Dog:
CHINOOK

WACKY FACT!
The very first potato was planted in New Hampshire!

29

New Jersey

State Capital:
TRENTON

State Fish:
BROOK TROUT

State Animal:
HORSE

WACKY FACT!
New Jersey is the Diner Capital of the World!

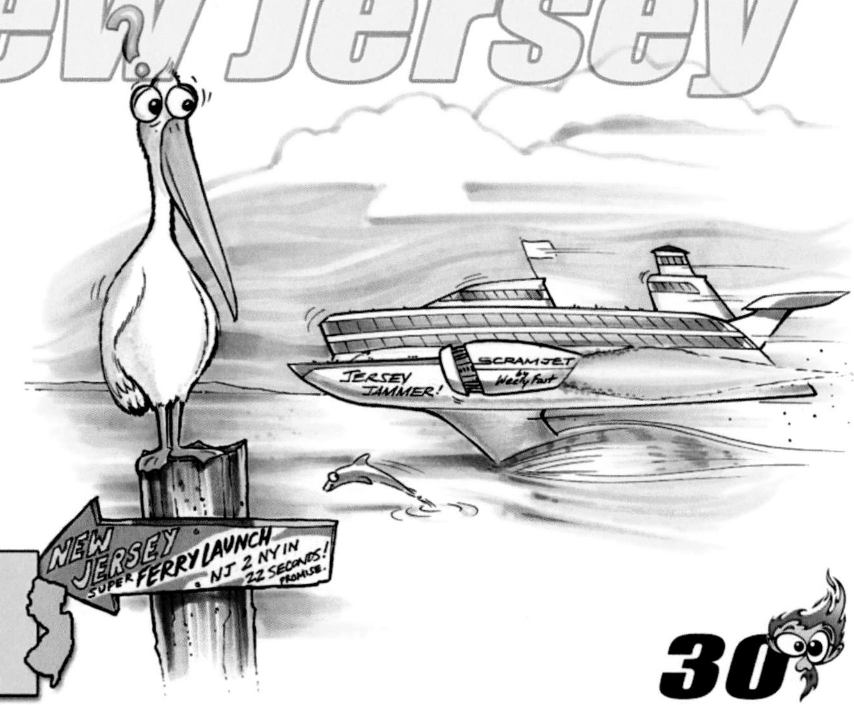
NEW JERSEY SUPER FERRY LAUNCH
NJ 2 NY IN 22 SECONDS!
PROMISE.
JERSEY JAMMER!
SCRAMJET
by Wacky Fast
30

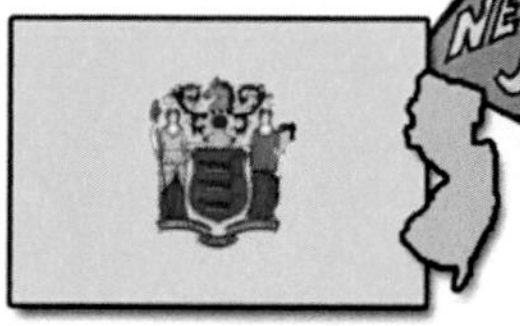

New Mexico

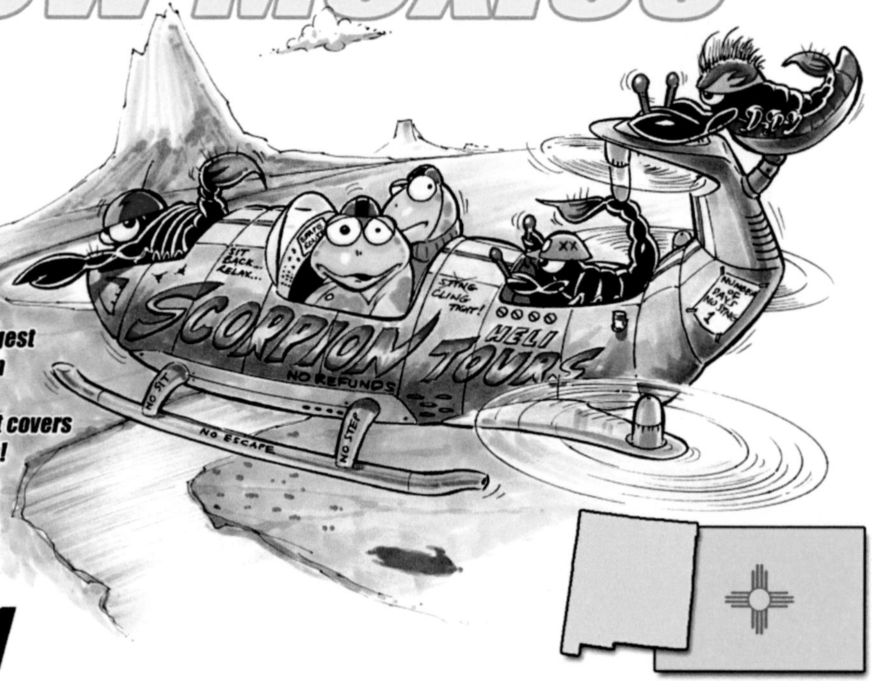
SCORPION
HELI
TOURS
NO REFUNDS
NO ESCAPE
NO STEP
NO SIT
SIT BACK... RELAX...
STING CLING TIGHT!
NUMBER OF DAYS NO STING 1

State Capital:
SANTA FE

State Animal:
TARANTULA HAWK WASP

WACKY FACT!
The Navajo, the Nation's largest Native American Group, have a reservation that covers 14 million Acres!

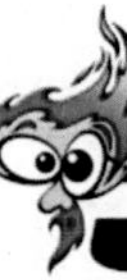

31

New York

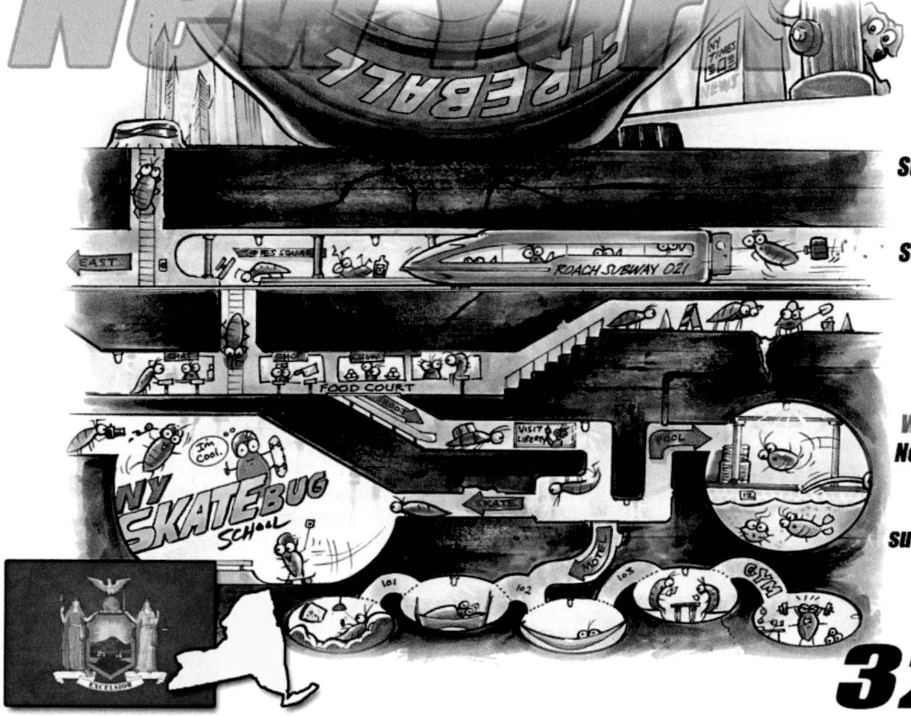
FIREBALL
NY TIMES
NEWS
EAST
ROACH SUBWAY 021
FOOD COURT
VISIT LIBERTY
POOL
I'm cool.
NY SKATEBUG SCHOOL
SKATE
MOTEL
101
102
103
GYM
EXCELSIOR

State Capital:
ALBANY

State Animal:
BEAVER

State Fruit:
APPLE

WACKY FACT!
New York City has 722 miles of subway track!

32

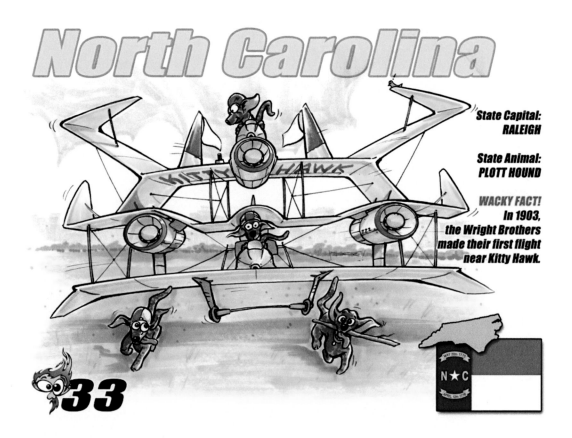

North Carolina
State Capital:
RALEIGH
State Animal:
PLOTT HOUND
WACKY FACT!
In 1903,
the Wright Brothers
made their first flight
near Kitty Hawk.
KITTY HAWK
33
N★C
MAY 20th 1775
APRIL 12th 1776

North Dakota

STEAM
103
NUTTER
NORTH DAKOTA
34

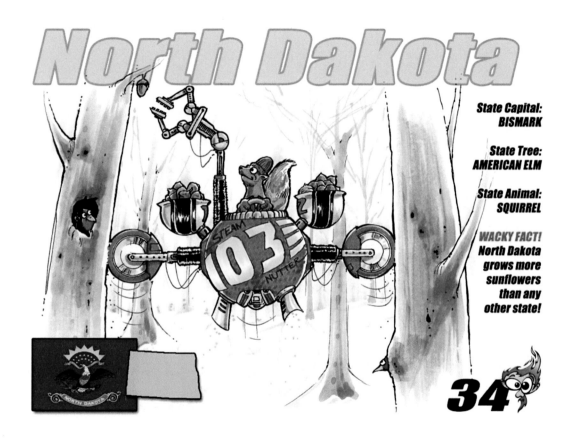

State Capital:
BISMARK

State Tree:
AMERICAN ELM

State Animal:
SQUIRREL

WACKY FACT!
North Dakota grows more sunflowers than any other state!

Ohio

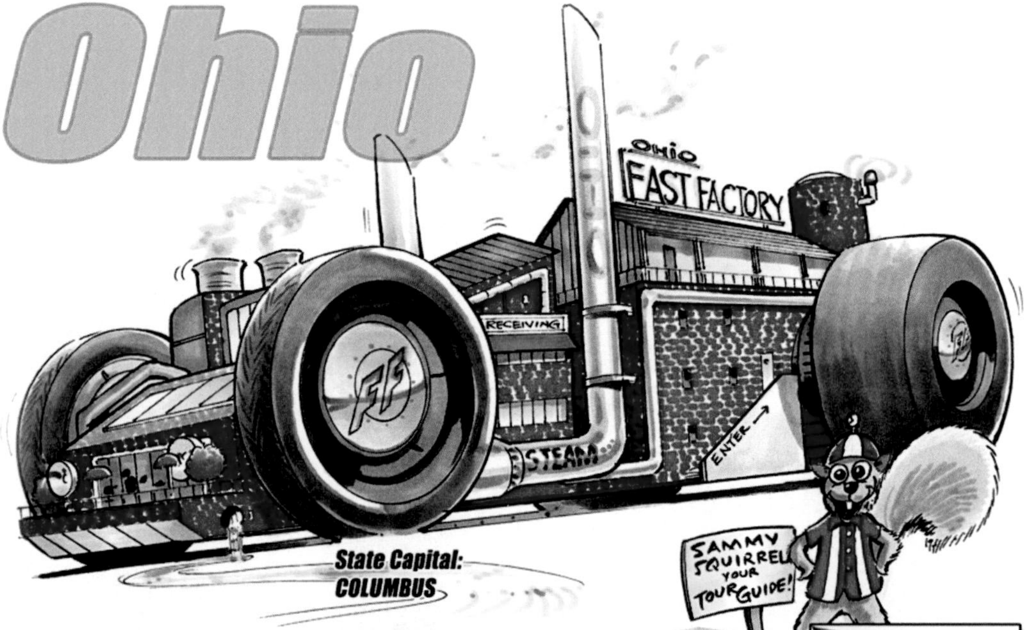
OHIO
FAST FACTORY
RECEIVING
STEAM
ENTER →
SAMMY SQUIRREL YOUR TOUR GUIDE!

State Capital:
COLUMBUS

State Tree:
OHIO BUCKEYE

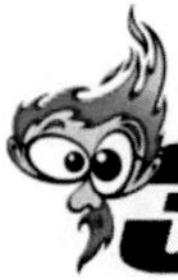

35

WACKY FACT! Cleveland boasts America's first traffic light in 1914!

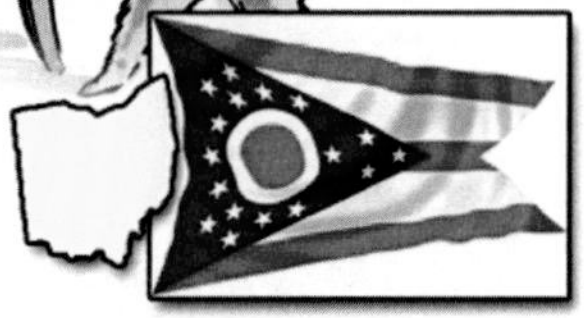

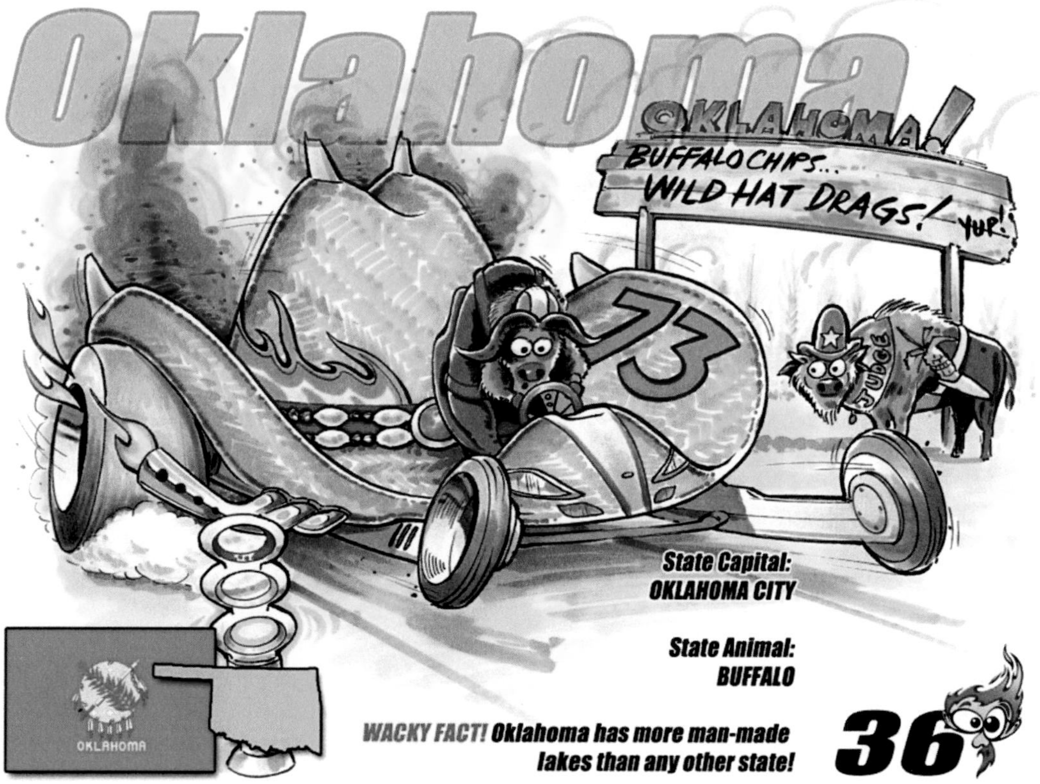
Oklahoma
OKLAHOMA!
BUFFALO CHIPS...
WILD HAT DRAGS!
YUP!
73
JUDGE
OKLAHOMA
State Capital:
OKLAHOMA CITY
State Animal:
BUFFALO
WACKY FACT! Oklahoma has more man-made lakes than any other state!
36

Oregon

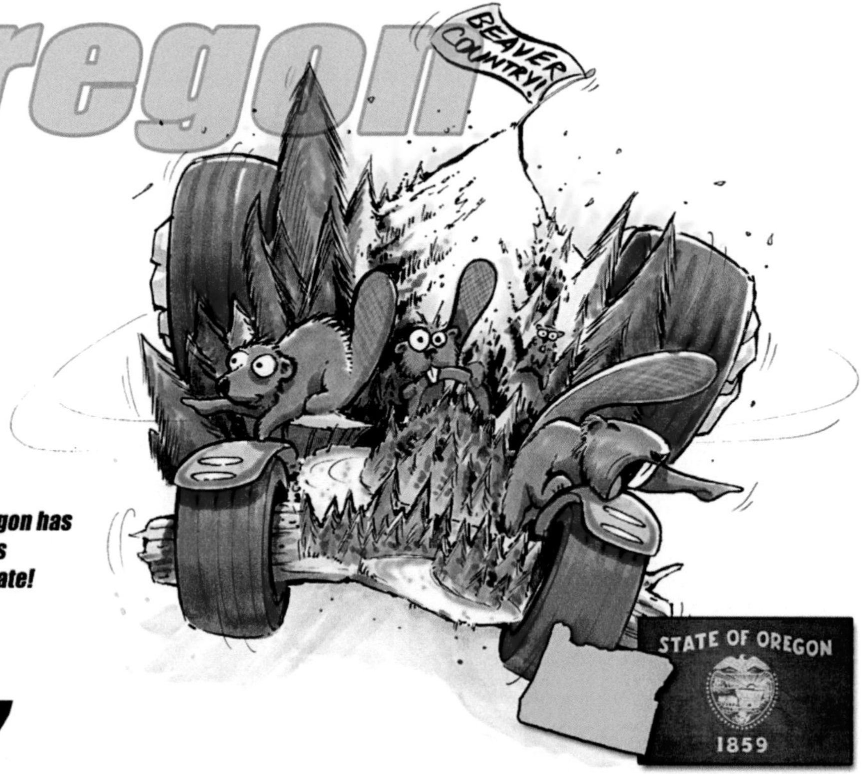
BEAVER COUNTRY!
STATE OF OREGON
1859

State Capital:
SALEM

State Animal:
BEAVER

State Fruit:
PEAR

State Flower:
OREGON GRAPE

WACKY FACT! Oregon has more ghost towns than any other state!

37

Pennsylvania

State Capital:
HARRISBURG

State Dog:
THE GREAT DANE

WACKY FACT! Hershey, PA is considered the Chocolate Capital of the United States!

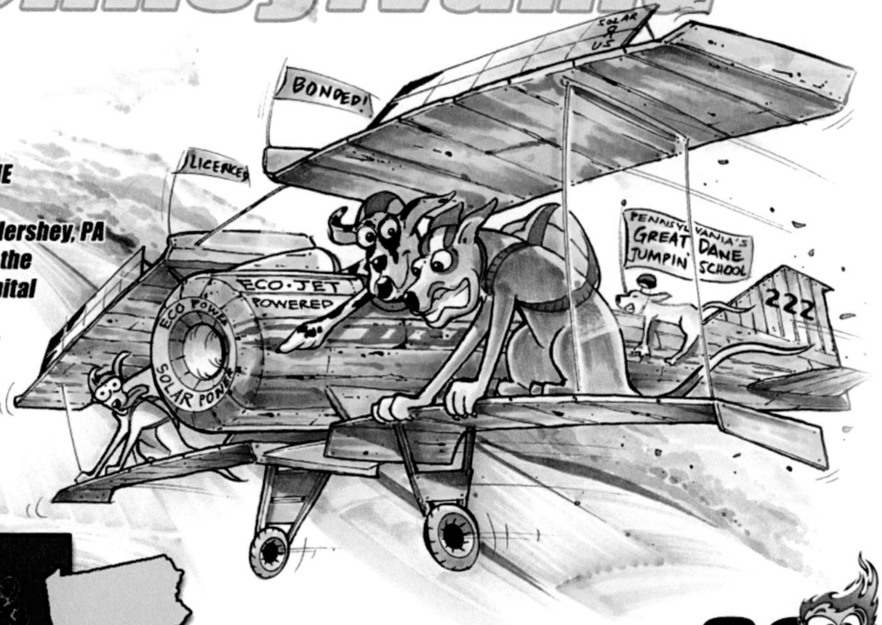
BONDED!
LICENCED
ECO-JET
POWERED
ECO POWER
SOLAR POWER
PENNSYLVANIA'S GREAT DANE JUMPIN' SCHOOL
222

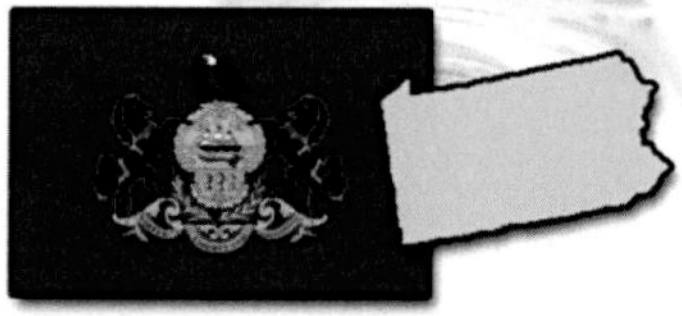

38

Rhode Island

State Capital:
PROVIDENCE

State Tree:
MAPLE

WACKY FACT!
Rhode Island is the
smallest state in
the United States!

39

South Carolina

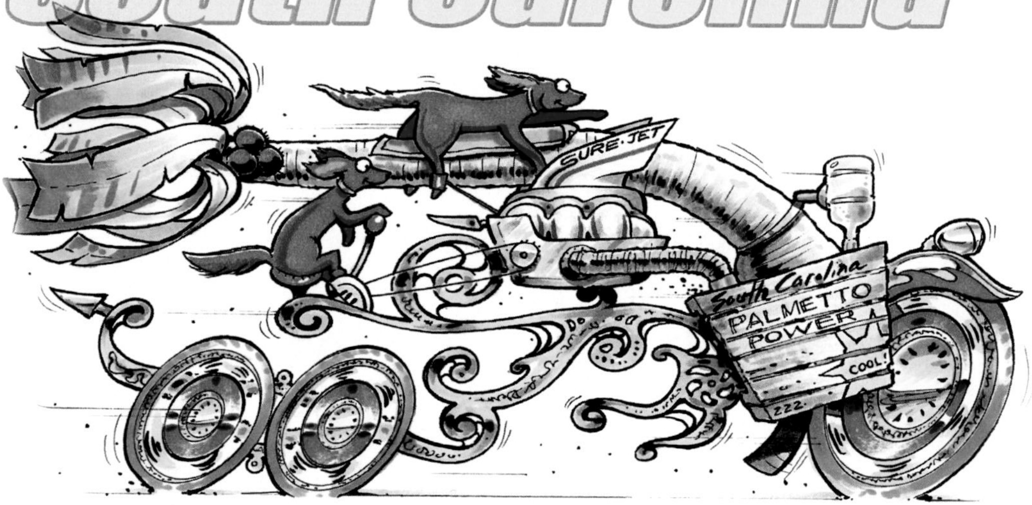
SURE JET
South Carolina
PALMETTO
POWER
COOL!

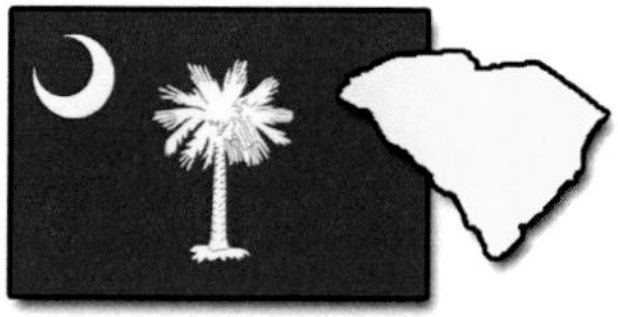

State Capital: COLUMBIA

State Dog: BOYKIN SPANIEL

WACKY FACT! The Salamander is the Official State Amphibian!

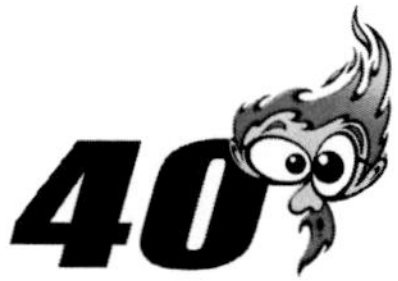
40

South Dakota

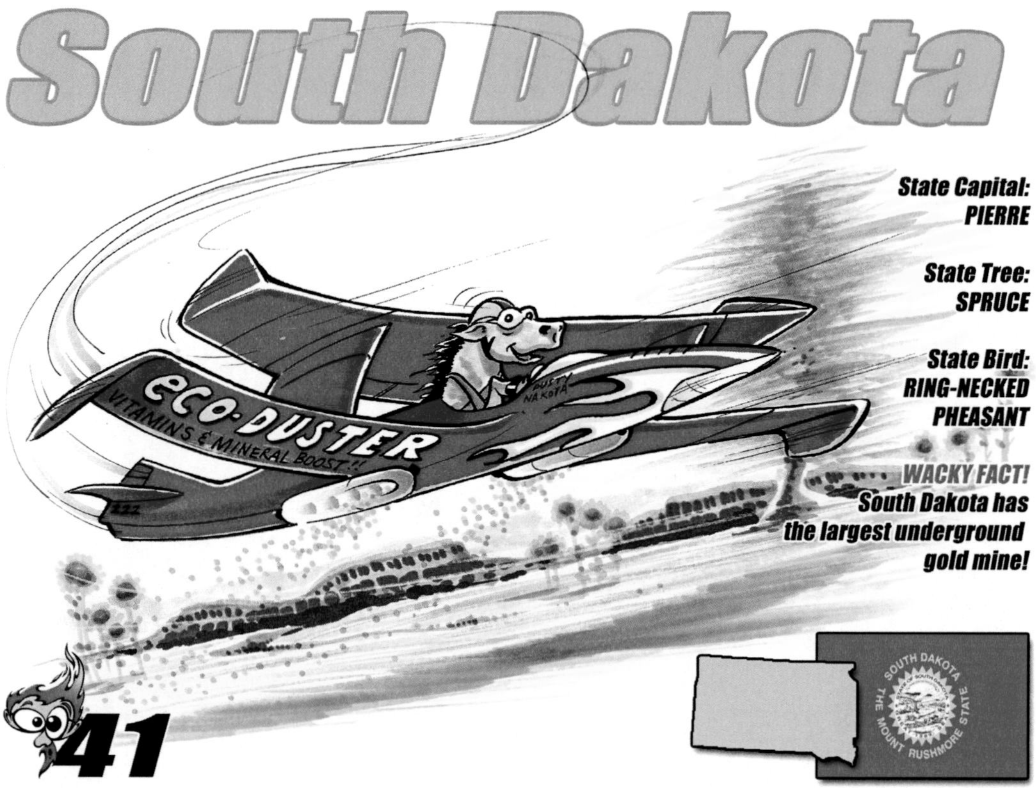
State Capital:
PIERRE
State Tree:
SPRUCE
State Bird:
RING-NECKED
PHEASANT
WACKY FACT!
South Dakota has
the largest underground
gold mine!
eco-DUSTER
VITAMINS & MINERAL BOOST!!
DUSTY NAKOTA
SOUTH DAKOTA
THE MOUNT RUSHMORE STATE
41

Tennessee

State Capital:
NASHVILLE

State Insect:
LADY BUG

WACKY FACT! Tennessee is the Turtle Capital of the World!

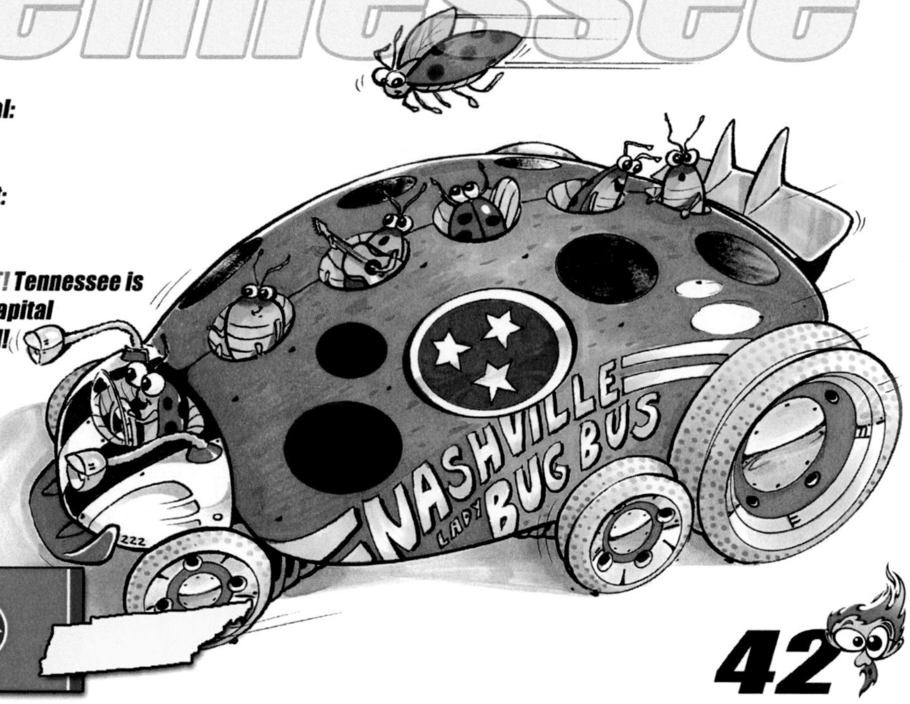
NASHVILLE
LADY BUG BUS
ZZZ
42

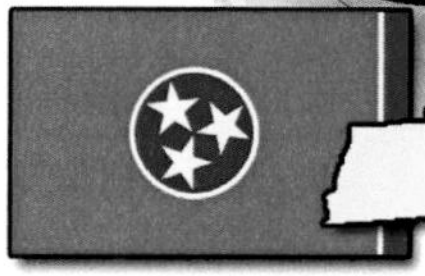

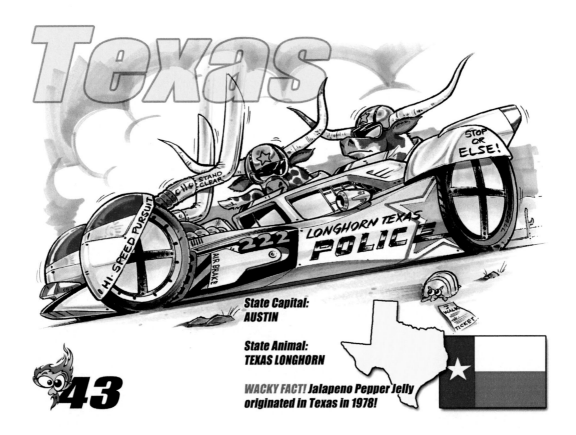

Texas
STAND CLEAR
HI-SPEED PURSUIT
222
AIR BRAKE
LONGHORN TEXAS
POLICE
STOP OR ELSE!
J WALK TICKET
State Capital:
AUSTIN
State Animal:
TEXAS LONGHORN
WACKY FACT! Jalapeno Pepper Jelly
originated in Texas in 1978!
43

Utah
State Capital:
SALT LAKE CITY
State Animal:
ROCKY MOUNTAIN ELK
WACKY FACT! Utah has five national parks: Arches, Canyonlands, Zion, Bryce and Capitol Reef!
ROCKY'S BRYCE ROCKETROCK TOUR!
INDUSTRY
UTAH
1896
44

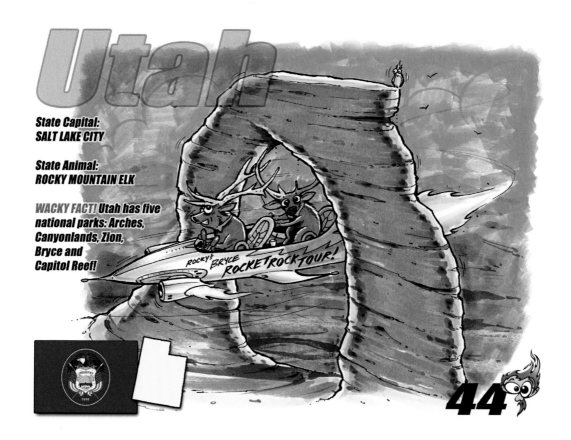

Vermont

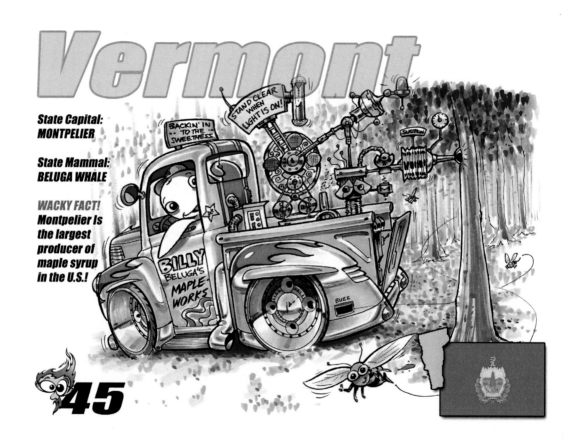

State Capital:
MONTPELIER

State Mammal:
BELUGA WHALE

WACKY FACT!
Montpelier Is the largest producer of maple syrup in the U.S.!

BACKIN' IN TO THE SWEETNESS
STAND CLEAR WHEN LIGHT IS ON!
SUCTION
BILLY BELUGA'S MAPLE WORKS
BUZZ

45

Virginia

VIRGINIA
1788
2088
URIBUS UNUM

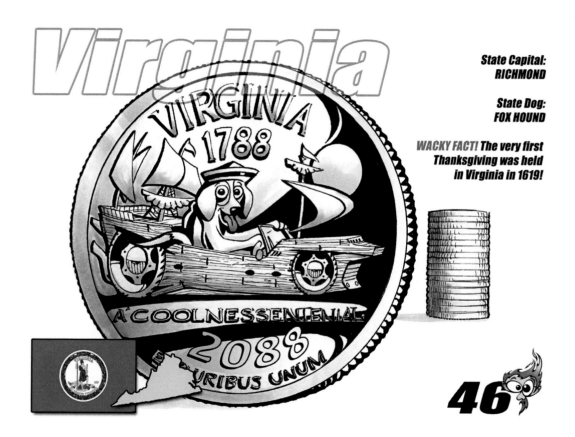

State Capital:
RICHMOND

State Dog:
FOX HOUND

***WACKY FACT!* The very first Thanksgiving was held in Virginia in 1619!**

46

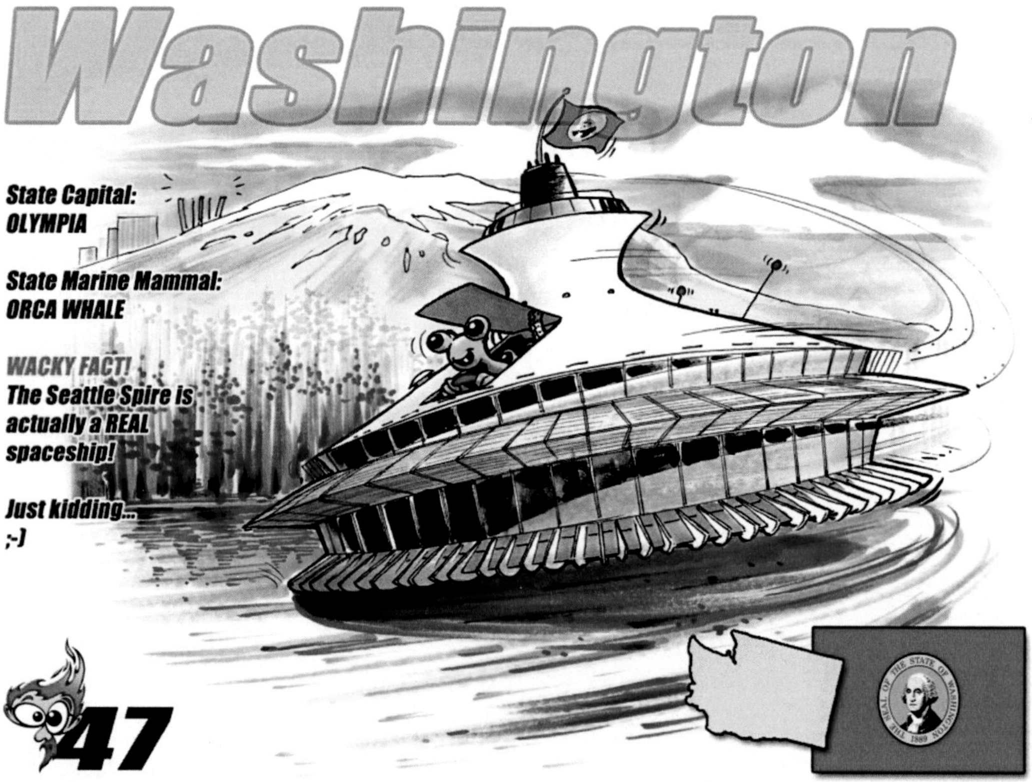
Washington
State Capital:
OLYMPIA
State Marine Mammal:
ORCA WHALE
WACKY FACT!
The Seattle Spire is actually a REAL spaceship!
Just kidding...
;-)
47
THE SEAL OF THE STATE OF WASHINGTON 1889

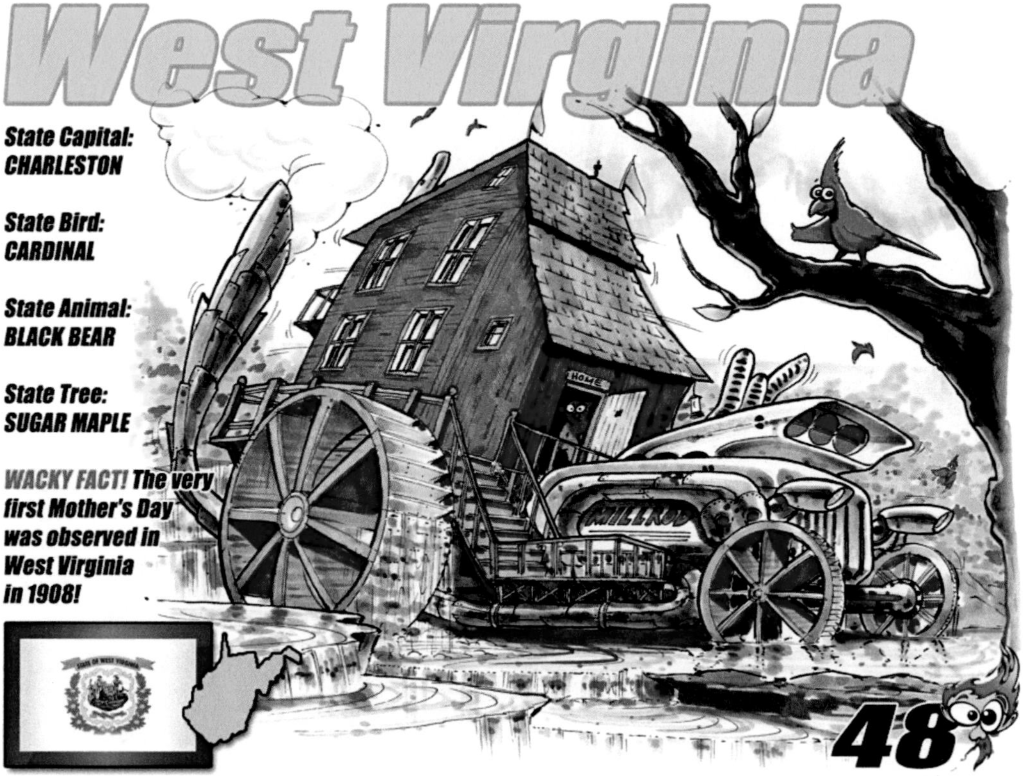
West Virginia
State Capital:
CHARLESTON
State Bird:
CARDINAL
State Animal:
BLACK BEAR
State Tree:
SUGAR MAPLE
WACKY FACT! The very first Mother's Day was observed in West Virginia in 1908!
HOME
48

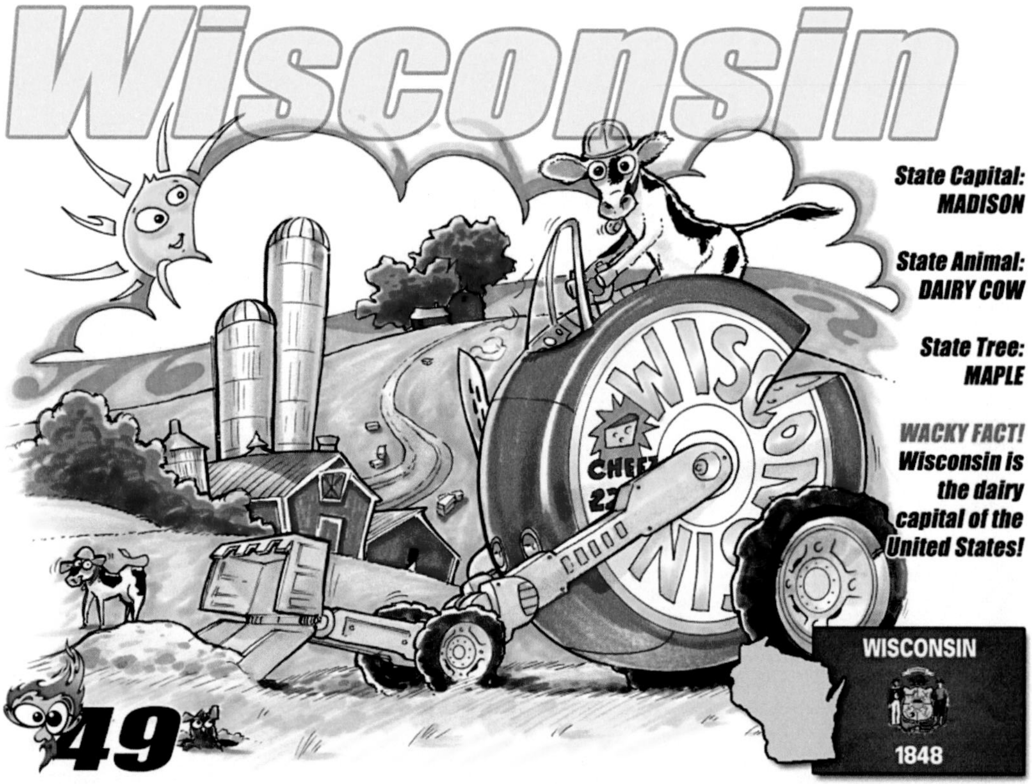
Wisconsin
State Capital:
MADISON
State Animal:
DAIRY COW
State Tree:
MAPLE
WACKY FACT!
Wisconsin is the dairy capital of the United States!
WISCONSIN
WISCONSIN
1848
49

Wyoming

State Capital:
CHEYENNE

State Tree:
COTTONWOOD

State Bird:
WESTERN MEADOWLARK

WACKY FACT! Devil's Tower was the very first National Monument in 1906!

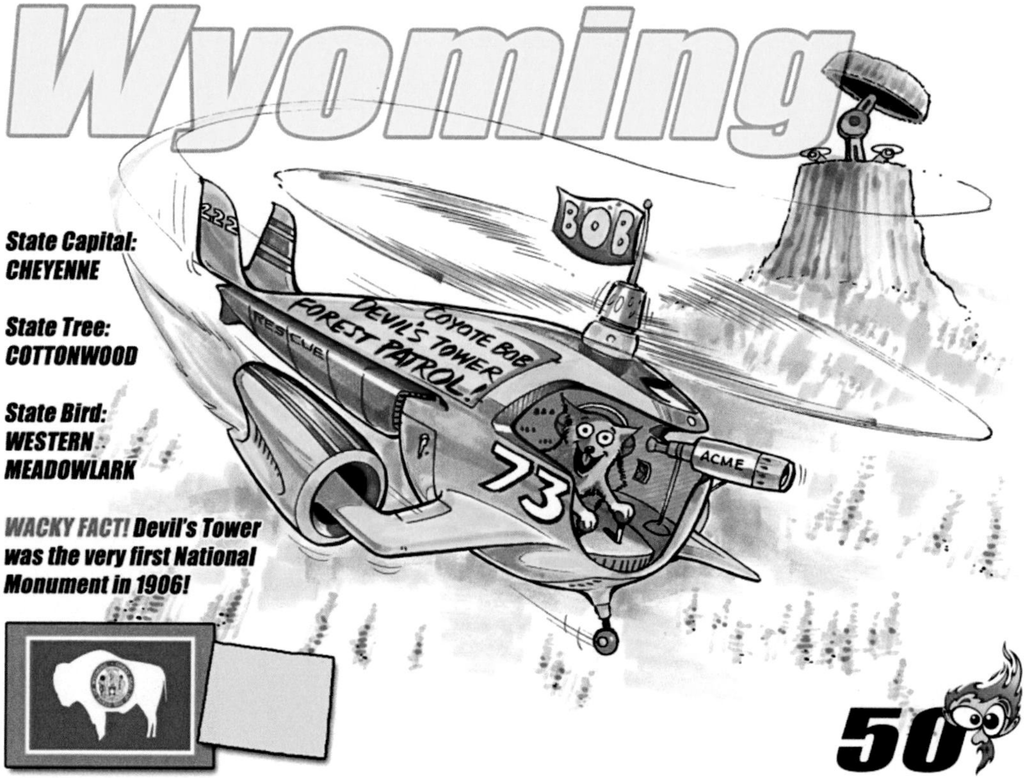
Wyoming
BOB
COYOTE BOB
DEVIL'S TOWER
FOREST PATROL!
RESCUE
222
73
ACME
50

ABOUT THE AUTHOR

Fireball Tim Lawrence is a Hollywood TV Host, Movie Car Designer, Cartoonist & Author.

For more information visit
http://www.fireballtim.com

Made in the USA
San Bernardino, CA
21 November 2015